MW00564032

Famous & Fun Duets

6 Duets for One Piano, Four Hands

Carol Matz

Famous & Fun Duets, Book 3, contains carefully selected familiar songs and timeless masterworks of the great composers. The duets are arranged in equal parts for elementary to late-elementary pianists, and are written for one piano, four hands. For easier reading, each part is written using both treble and bass clefs, with directions for the *primo* to play up an octave and the *secondo* down an octave. Additionally, the melody often shifts between *primo* and *secondo,* creating interesting parts for both players. Students are sure to enjoy their experience with these fun duets!

Alfred Music Publishing Co., Inc.
P.O. Box 10003
Van Nuys, CA 91410-0003
alfred.com

Copyright © MMX by Alfred Music Publishing Co., Inc.
All rights reserved. Printed in USA.

No part of this book shall be reproduced, arranged, adapted, recorded, publicly performed, stored in a retrieval system,
or transmitted by any means without written permission from the publisher. In order to comply with copyright laws, please apply for
such written permission and/or license by contacting the publisher at alfred.com/permissions.

ISBN-10: 0-7390-7651-5
ISBN-13: 978-0-7390-7651-4

Spring

(from *The Four Seasons*)

Secondo

Antonio Vivaldi
Arranged by Carol Matz

Lively

Play both hands one octave lower

Spring

(from *The Four Seasons*)

Primo

Antonio Vivaldi
Arranged by Carol Matz

Lively
Play both hands one octave higher

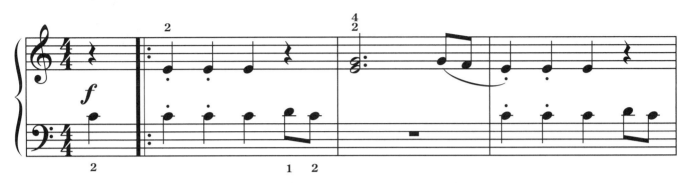

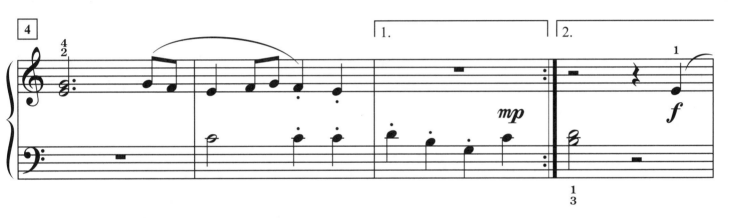

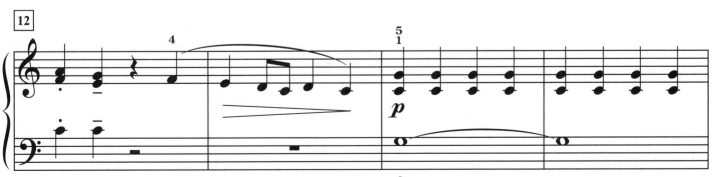

Secondo

Primo

Yankee Doodle Dandy

(from the musical film *Yankee Doodle Dandy*)

Secondo

George M. Cohan
Arranged by Carol Matz

Brightly
Play both hands one octave lower

Yankee Doodle Dandy

(from the musical film *Yankee Doodle Dandy*)

Primo

George M. Cohan
Arranged by Carol Matz

Brightly
Play both hands one octave higher

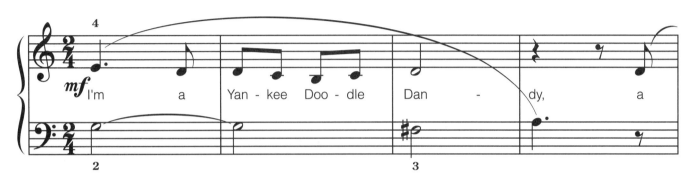

I'm a Yan - kee Doo - dle Dan - dy, a

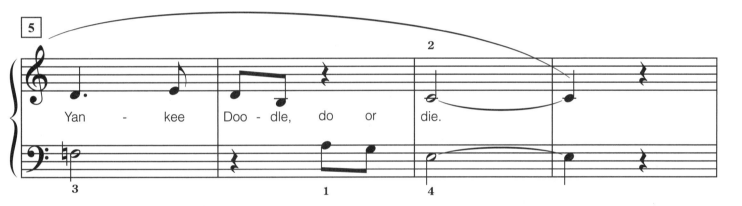

Yan - kee Doo - dle, do or die.

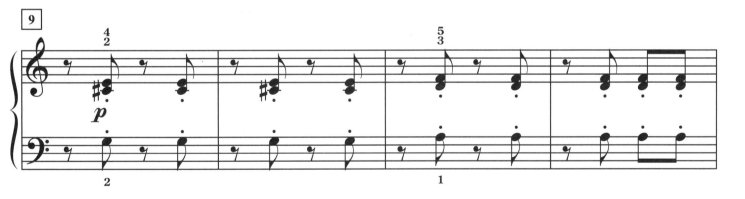

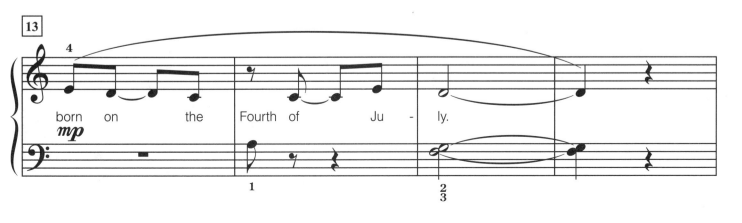

born on the Fourth of Ju - ly.

Secondo

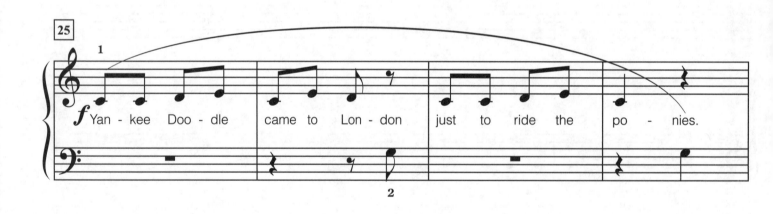

Yan - kee Doo - dle   came to Lon - don   just to ride the   po - nies.

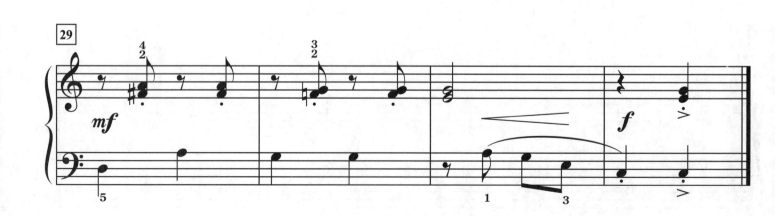

Primo

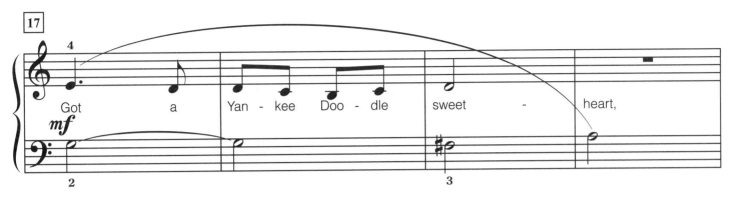

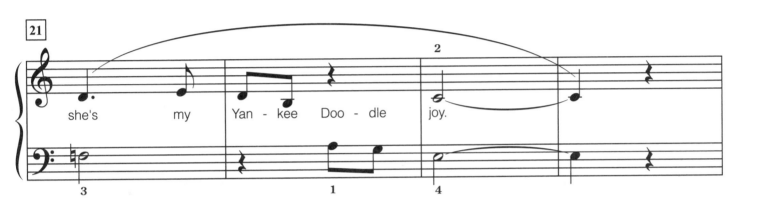

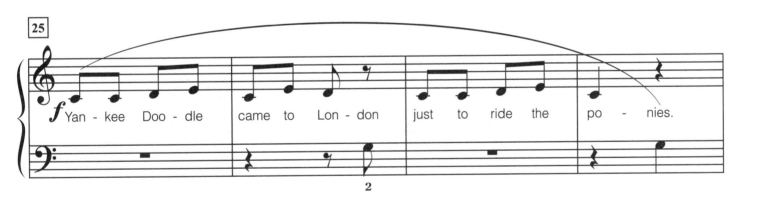

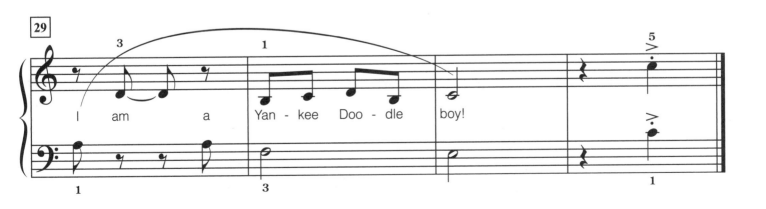

America

(My Country, 'Tis of Thee)

Secondo

Henry Carey
Words by Samuel F. Smith
Arranged by Carol Matz

Moderately
Play both hands one octave lower

My coun - try, 'tis of thee, sweet land of lib - er - ty,

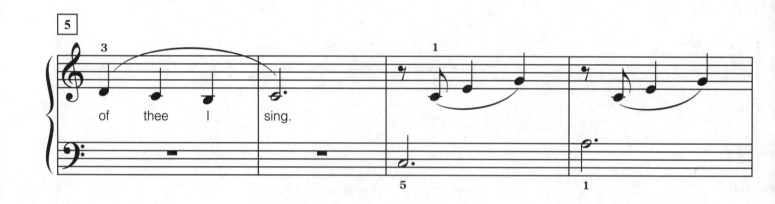

of thee I sing.

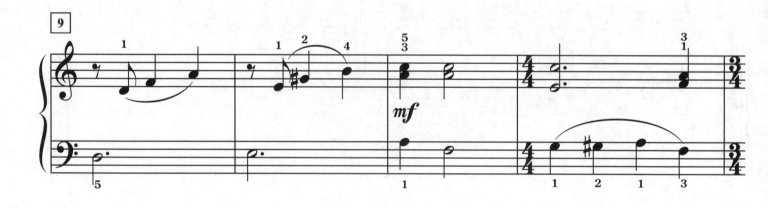

America

(My Country, 'Tis of Thee)

Primo

Henry Carey
Words by Samuel F. Smith
Arranged by Carol Matz

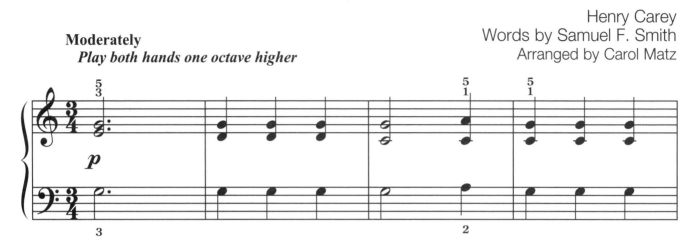

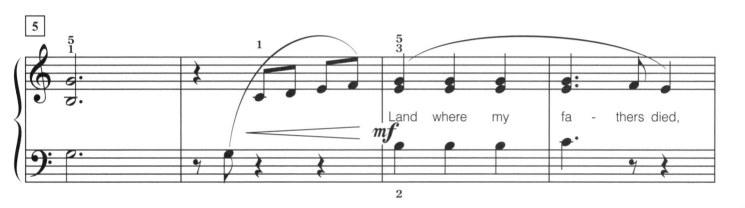

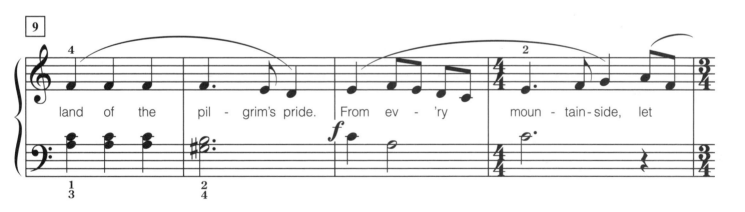

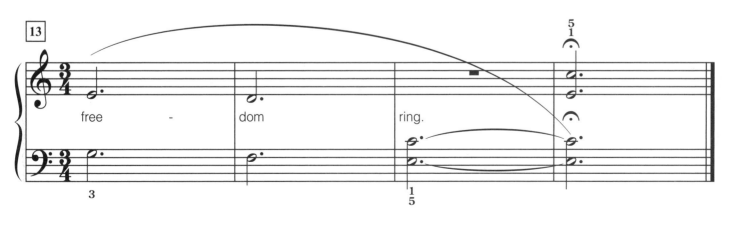

Overture to The Barber of Seville

(from the opera *The Barber of Seville*)

Secondo

Gioachino Rossini
Arranged by Carol Matz

Moderately fast
Play both hands one octave lower

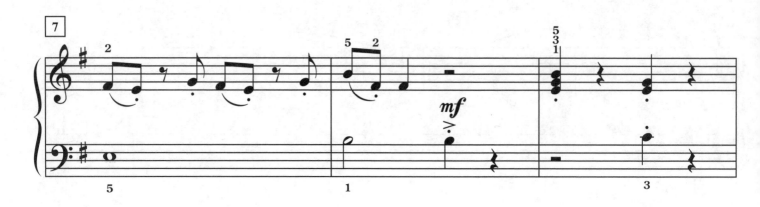

Overture to The Barber of Seville

(from the opera *The Barber of Seville*)

Primo

Gioachino Rossini
Arranged by Carol Matz

Moderately fast
Play both hands one octave higher

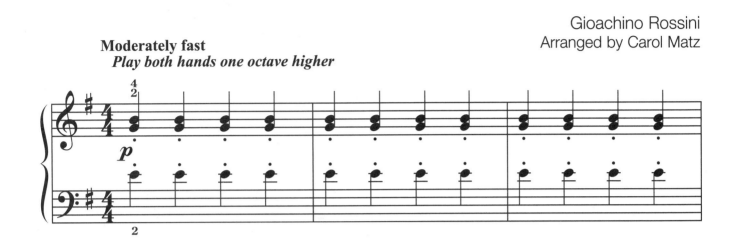

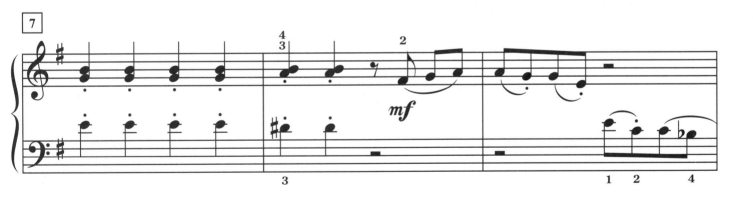

Secondo

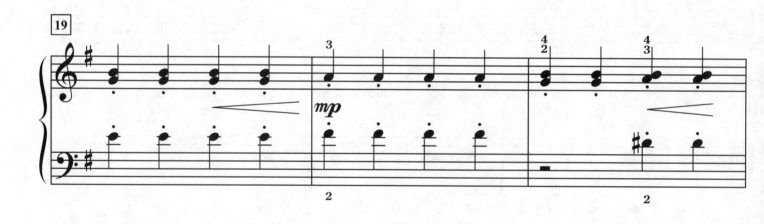

Primo

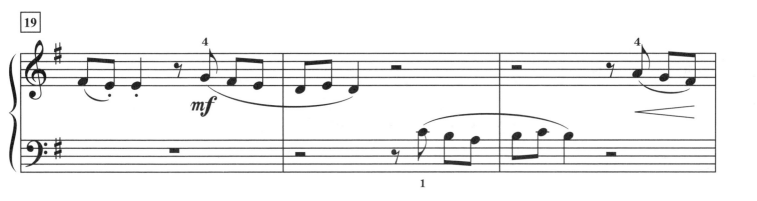

Dance of the Hours

(from the opera *La Gioconda*)

Secondo

Amilcare Ponchielli
Arranged by Carol Matz

Moderately fast
Play both hands one octave lower

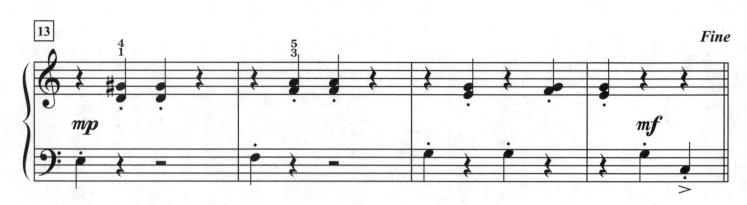

Dance of the Hours

(from the opera *La Gioconda*)

Primo

Amilcare Ponchielli
Arranged by Carol Matz

Moderately fast
Play both hands one octave higher

Secondo

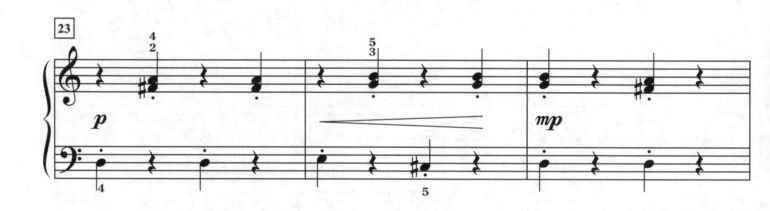

D.C. al Fine

Primo

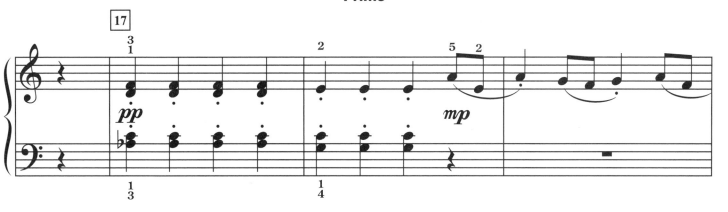

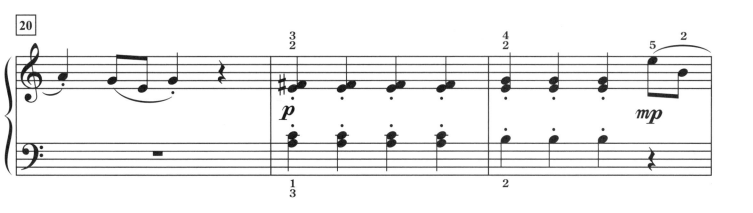

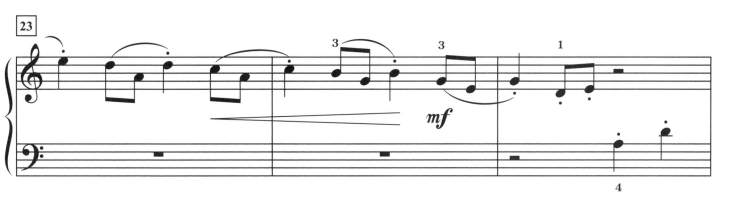

D.C. al Fine

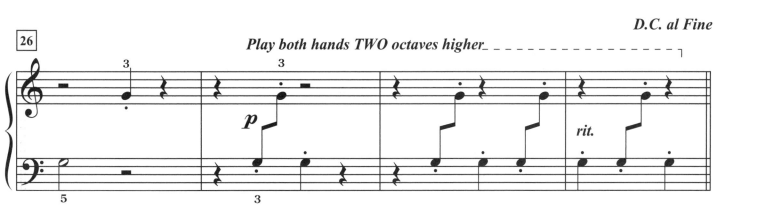

Gymnopédie I

Secondo

Erik Satie
Arranged by Carol Matz

Gymnopédie I

Primo

Erik Satie
Arranged by Carol Matz

Moderately slow
Play both hands TWO octaves higher

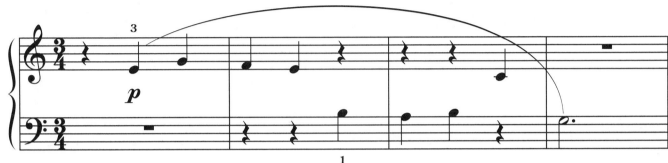

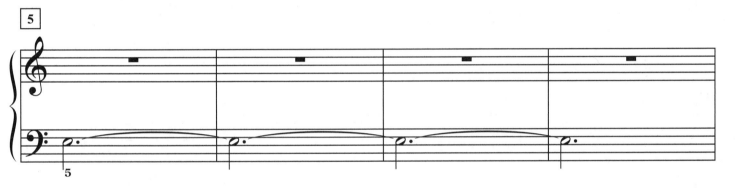

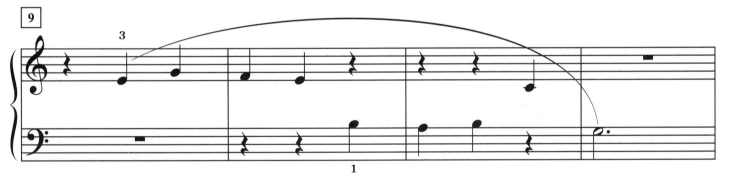

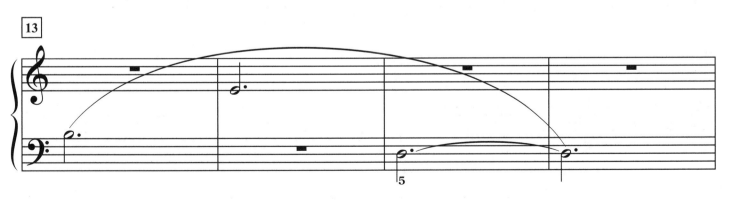

Secondo

Primo

Play both hands ONE octave higher to the end

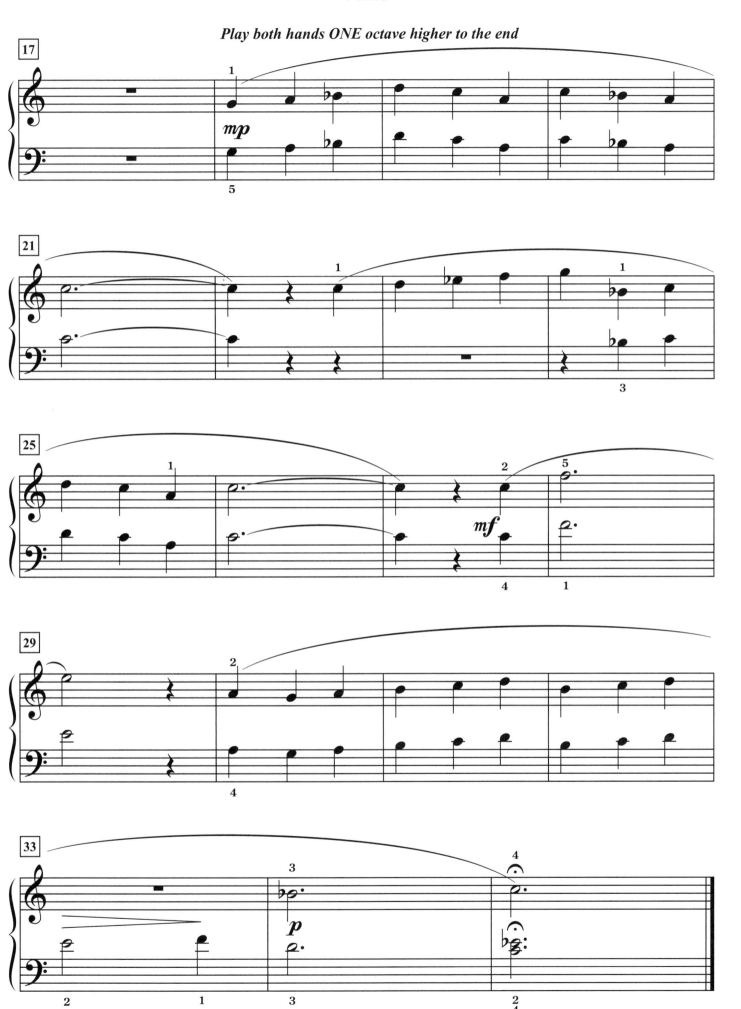